OFFICIAL BATTING ORDER

ST. LOUIS

DATE __8/28/3__

	ORIGINAL			CHANGE	ALSO ELIGIBLE
1				B 3-2 F	Cairo
				C HR	Benz
2				B	Taguchi
				C	Wedge
3				B	
				C	
4				B	Palmeiro
				C	
5				B	
				C HR	
6				B	Halpen/8
				C	
7				B	
				C	
8				B	Fssro
				C	
9				B	Klein/8 ✓Klein
				C	Taguchi/8
				D	
				E	Eldred

MANAGER'S SIGNATURE --

THREE NIGHTS IN AUGUST

BOOKS BY BUZZ BISSINGER

Friday Night Lights • *A Prayer for the City* • *Three Nights in August*

The Best American Sports Writing 2003 (editor)

THREE NIGHTS
IN AUGUST

Strategy, Heartbreak, and Joy

Inside the Mind of a Manager

Buzz Bissinger

HOUGHTON MIFFLIN COMPANY

Boston • New York • 2005

For information about permission to reproduce selections from this book, write to Permissions, Houghton Mifflin Company, 215 Park Avenue South, New York, New York 10003.

Visit our Web site: www.houghtonmifflinbooks.com.

Library of Congress Cataloging-in-Publication Data

Bissinger, H. G.
    Three nights in August / Buzz Bissinger.
        p.   cm.
    ISBN 0-618-40544-5
        1. St. Louis Cardinals (Baseball team) 2. Chicago Cubs (Baseball team) 3. La Russa, Tony. I. Title.
    GV875.S74B57   2005
    796.357'09778'66—dc22   2004065134

Book design by Melissa Lotfy

PRINTED IN THE UNITED STATES OF AMERICA

QUM 10 9 8 7 6 5 4 3 2 1

To Lisa, Caleb, and Maddy.
A beautiful woman. A beautiful son. A beautiful friend.

—HGB

● ● ●

To Elaine, Bianca, and Devon, and the four-legged companions who have been part of our family. They mean more to me than they did yesterday and less than they will tomorrow.

And to the baseball family—those I have competed with and those I have competed against.

—TLR

I'm as nauseous as I've ever been. I have a terrible headache. My head is pounding. I feel like throwing up and I'm having trouble swallowing. And the beauty of it is, you want to feel like this every day.

—Tony La Russa

CONTENTS

GAME THREE

PREFACE

● ● ● THE FACE made me do it. It left an indelible image with its eternal glower from the dark corner that it occupied. I had always admired intensity in others, but the face of Tony La Russa entered a new dimension, nothing quite like it in all of sports.

I first saw the face in the early 1980s, when La Russa came out of nowhere at the age of thirty-four to manage the Chicago White Sox and took them to a division championship in his third full year of managing. The face simply smoldered; it could have been used as a welding tool or rented out to a tanning salon. A few years later, when he managed the Oakland A's to the World Series three times in a row, the face was a regular fixture on network television and raised even more questions in my mind. Did it *ever* crack a smile? Did it *ever* relax? Did it *ever* loosen up and let down the guard a little bit, even in the orgy of victory? As far I could tell, the answer was no.

I was hooked on the face. I continued to observe it as he stayed with the Oakland A's through 1995. I followed it when he became the manager of the St. Louis Cardinals the following season. Along the way, I became aware of his reputation as a manager, with a polarity of opinion over him such that when *Sports Illustrated* polled players on the game's best five managers and its worst five managers, La Russa appeared on both lists. But I liked seeing that because it meant to me that this was a manager who didn't hold back, who ran his club with a distinct style regardless of the critics' chorus. Had he been any different, surely the face would have broken into a smile at least *once*.

After La Russa came to the Cardinals, I did see moments when the face changed. I saw fatherly pride and self-effacement spread over it when Mark McGwire hit his record-breaking sixty-second home run in 1998. I also saw the face overcome with grief when he and his coaches and his players mourned the passing of the soul of the St. Louis Cardinals, broadcast announcer Jack Buck, followed four days later by the death of beloved pitcher Darryl Kile in his hotel room during a road trip in Chicago. Later that season of 2002, I saw the intensity return, all the features on a collision course to the same hard line across the lips during the National League Championship series that the Cardinals painfully lost to the Giants four games to one.

As a lifelong baseball fan, I found myself more curious about La Russa than about anybody else in the game. Which is why, when out of nowhere, I received a call from La Russa's agent at the end of November 2002 asking whether I might be interested in collaborating on a book with La Russa, my answer was an immediate yes. I jumped at the opportunity, although I also knew that collaborations can be a tricky business. I had been offered them before by the likes of Rudy Giuliani and legendary television producer Roone Arledge, and I had turned them down. But this was different, or at least I told myself it was different, because—at the risk of sounding like some field-of-dreams idiot—my love of baseball has been perhaps the greatest single constant of my life. I knew the game as a fan, which is a wonderful way to know it. But the opportunity to know it through the mind of La Russa—to excavate deep into the game and try to capture the odd and lonely corner of the dugout that he and all managers occupy by virtue of the natural isolation of their craft—was simply too good to pass up.

In the beginning, this was a typical collaboration. I brought along my little mini–cassette recorder to where La Russa lived in northern California. I turned it on and interviewed him at length, thinking that I would listen to the tapes and transcribe them and try to fashion what he said into his own voice. As is common in collaborations, we also have a business arrangement, a split of the proceeds, although the entirety of La Russa's share is going to the Animal Rescue Foundation, known as Tony La Russa's ARF, that he cofounded with his wife, Elaine, in northern California.

The more we talked about the book, the more agreement there was about trying to do something different from the typical as-told-to. La Russa's interest in me as a writer had been on the basis of *Friday Night Lights,* a book I had written about high school football in Texas. He was struck by the voice and observational qualities of the book, and we wondered whether there was a way to fashion that here. We also wondered whether there was a way to write the book with a narrative structure different from the usual season-in-the-life trajectory, a book that would have lasting and universal application no matter what season it took place in.

It was during those conversations that we came up with the idea of crafting the book around the timeless unit of baseball, the three-game series. The one we settled on, against the eternal rival Chicago Cubs, took place in the 2003 season. Had the goal of the book been different—to write about a particular season—it would have made sense to switch gears and write about the Cardinals' magnificent ride of 2004. But that wasn't the goal.

It was also during those conversations that La Russa agreed to give me virtually unlimited access to the Cardinals' clubhouse and the coaches and players and personnel who populate it—not simply for the three-game series that forms the spine of the book but also for the virtual entirety of the 2003 season—to soak up the subculture as much as possible. La Russa understood that in granting such access, he was ceding much of the control of the book to me as its writer. In doing so, he was untying the usual constraints of a collaboration, allowing me wide latitude to report and observe and draw my own conclusions. He also knew that approaching the book in this manner required him to be revealing of not only the strategies he has come to use but also the wrenching personal compromises he has made in order to be the kind of manager he has chosen to be.

La Russa did not waver from the latitude that he promised. I was made privy to dozens of private meetings between the Cardinals coaches and their players. I was able to roam the clubhouse freely. Because of my access, I was also able to probe not only La Russa's mind but also the minds of so many others who populate a clubhouse. La Russa has read what I have written—the place where collaborations can get odious. He has clarified, but in no place has he asked that anything be removed, no matter how candid.

I came into this book as an admirer of La Russa. I leave with even more admiration not simply because of the intellectual complexity with which he reaches his decisions but also because of the place that I believe he occupies in the changing world of baseball.

He seems like a vanishing breed to me, in the same way that Joe Torre of the New York Yankees and Bobby Cox of Atlanta and Lou Piniella of Tampa Bay also seem like the last of their kind. They so clearly love the game. They revel in the history of it. They have values as fine as they are old-fashioned, and they have combined them with the belief that a manager's role is to be shrewd and aggressive and intuitive, that the job is more about unlocking the hearts of players than the mere deciphering of their statistics.

In the fallout of Michael Lewis's provocative book *Moneyball,* baseball front offices are increasingly being populated by thirty-somethings whose most salient qualifications are MBA degrees and who come equipped with a clinical ruthlessness: The skills of players don't even have to be observed but instead can be diagnosed by adept statistical analysis through a computer. These thirtysomethings view players as pieces of an assembly line; the goal is to quantify the inefficiencies that are slowing down production and then to improve on it with cost-effective player parts.

In this new wave of baseball, managers are less *managers* than *middle managers,* functionaries whose strategic options during a game require muzzlement, there only to effect the marching orders coldly calculated and passed down by upper management. It is wrong to say that the new breed doesn't care about baseball. But it's not wrong to say that there is no way they could possibly *love* it, and so much of baseball is about love. They don't have the sense of history, which to the thirtysomethings is largely bunk. They don't have the bus trips or the plane trips. They don't carry along the tradition, because they couldn't care less about the tradition. They have no use for the lore of the game—the poetry of its stories—because it can't be broken down and crunched into a computer. Just as they have no interest in the human ingredients that make a player a player and make a game a game: heart, desire, passion, reactions to pressure. After all, these are emotions, and what point are emotions if they can't be quantified?

La Russa is a baseball man, and he loves the appellation "baseball man." He loves the sound of it, although the term has become increasingly pejorative today because of the very stodginess that it suggests. But La Russa is not some hidebound manager stuck in the Dark Ages. He honors statistics and respects the studies that have been written about them. He pays meticulous attention to matchups. He thinks about slugging percentage and on-base percentage, as they have become the trendy statistics in today's game. They have a place in baseball, but he refuses to be held captive to them, because so much else has a place in baseball. Like Torre and Cox and Piniella, his history in the game makes him powerfully influenced by the very persuasions the thirtysomethings find so pointless: heart, desire, passion, reactions to pressure. After all, these are emotions, and what point is there playing baseball, or any game, if you don't celebrate them?

This book was not conceived as a response to *Moneyball.* Work began months before either La Russa or I had ever heard of Lewis's work. Nor is this book exclusively about La Russa. Because he is the manager, he is at the hub of the wheel of *Three Nights in August.* But the more time I spent in the clubhouse, the more aware I became of all the various spokes that emanate from that hub and make a team that thing called a team.

La Russa represents, to my mind, the best that baseball offers, but this book doesn't sidestep the less noble elements that have associated themselves with the game in the past few decades: the palpable decline in team spirit, the ever-escalating salaries, the burgeoning use of steroids—all are a part of what baseball has become. The sport has a tendency to cannibalize itself, to raise the bar of self-interest just when you thought it couldn't go any higher. The recent scandal of steroid abuse is shocking enough—with its lurid images of players lathering weird creams all over themselves—but what's truly shocking is that this problem has festered for at least a decade. As La Russa pointed out in one of our interviews, everybody in baseball knew for years that steroid use was taking place. But the only two powers that could have done something about it—the owners and the players' union—did nothing until 2002. It's difficult morally to understand that, but not financially, since steroids helped fuel the home-run craze that many who run baseball were convinced was the only way to capture new fans who lacked an interest in the game's subtleties.

It's a cynical notion and it's also wrong. Home runs are electrifying, but so are the dozens of smaller subplots that reveal themselves in every game, strategically and psychologically and emotionally. *Three Nights in August* tries to convey that very resonance, not with nostalgia, but because it is still the essence of this complex and layered game.

FOREWORD

BY TONY LA RUSSA

● ● ● IN THIS BOOK, Buzz Bissinger describes baseball as "complex and layered." I've been involved in professional baseball for over forty years, and the whole time I've been consumed by a drive to understand those complexities and layers. That process began in 1962, when at age seventeen I signed with Charley Finley's Kansas City Athletics. From the beginning of my playing career, "baseball men"—expert managers, coaches, scouts, and executives —tried to explain all the game's layers. They could break down each offensive and defensive play, for instance, showing how my responsibilities as a hitter could be different depending on the inning, score, and number of outs and base runners, if any. Early on, I started learning to "play the scoreboard"—that is, to figure out what play was appropriate at a given moment in the game and how to make it happen.

My education intensified dramatically in 1978, when I started managing the Knoxville Sox in the Double-A Southern League. As a player, your understanding of strategy and other subtleties is limited by the time and energy you must devote to the physical demands of playing. As a manager, however, your efforts to unlock the game's mysteries are no longer limited by physical constraints. You can apply yourself to this learning process during every play, every game—all the time.

By August 1979, I'd had only two partial seasons of minor-league managerial experience and one season in the winter league when Bill Veeck and Roland Hemond gave me an opportunity to manage the Chicago White Sox. At that time, the major leagues were populated largely by legendary managers—veterans so successful that they were recognized by their first names: Sparky, Billy, Earl, Gene, Chuck, Whitey, Tommy, Dick, and Johnny Mac. Against those managers and their teams, the White Sox and their new, thirty-four-year-old skipper were overmatched. To narrow that gap as much as possible, I grabbed at any information I could. Often, the information came from conversations with my legendary opponents, as well as other baseball men who generously shared their wisdom.

Twenty-five years on, I'm still learning. For example, as a former infielder, I'm less skilled at deciding what pitch to call in certain situations than somebody with a background as a pitcher or a catcher. Thousands of times over my two decades of working with pitching coach Dave Duncan, I've asked him what pitch to call. I still don't have Dave's expertise, but I'm getting better.

Aspects of the game that once baffled me—like where to position the defense in various game situations, or where to hit the ball with a runner on first and fewer than two outs (a hit to center or right beats a hit to left; a ground out beats a fly out if the runner is going on the pitch)—have become intelligible after exposure to dozens of expert tutors and postgame analysis of thousands of ballgames. Other mysteries remain. How can a quality team dominate during the regular season, win convincingly in the playoffs, but lose four straight or four of five in the World Series? That has happened to three teams I've managed: the A's in 1988 and 1990 and the 2004 Cardinals. I'm still searching for answers, and I don't like the one I'm left with: that when we suck it's mostly because I suck.

The more I've learned about baseball, the more my affection and respect for this beautiful game have grown. With that realization in mind, I decided several years ago that someday I'd like to be part of a book that described the intricate details of the game that baseball men (and, increasingly, women) have debated and passed along for over a century. Part of my motivation came from the many conversations I've had with fans who wanted to dig deeply into the layers. They would light up when we talked about the complexities of situational at-bats, defensive positioning, and pitching changes, or when we discussed the psychological nuances of the game, from the tactical value of getting a first-pitch strike (or ball, if you're a hitter) to the growing challenges of motivating extremely well-paid guys to put their team's success above their own.

I saw that for fans, too, deeper knowledge could mean greater pleasure. But how do you make inside baseball into a must-read book? I've always been a big reader, and I know that the nonfiction I like best is consistently entertaining, surprising, and honest. But I have enough trouble writing a lineup card, so I knew I had to find an author who could create a book with those qualities. People I respected recommended Buzz Bissinger, whose book *Friday Night Lights* I had enjoyed. Buzz agreed to the project and we had a collaboration going.

I quickly saw how truly gifted a writer Buzz is and how knowledgeable he is about baseball. As we worked together, Buzz's role gradually changed: Our collaboration became Buzz telling the story based on information he got from me and many others — managers, coaches, scouts, front-office people, and players — along with observations he made during a season spent watching the St. Louis Cardinals more closely than any writer has ever watched a ballclub before. All along, I've been aware of the contents of *Three Nights in August,* but it was Buzz who selected which people and events to feature and what stories to tell.

This book is about one three-game series between two teams in 2003. But Buzz and I agreed from the start that *Three Nights* should really be about baseball in general. Much of what you will read here would apply to any team at any time, in any season. My decisions and mistakes are mine alone, but all major-league managers have faced similar situations and have made similar decisions and similar mistakes. In much the same way, the players you'll read about here are particular people, but many of them also represent types of player: the clever veteran, the eager rookie, the spoiled star, the frustrated benchwarmer, the schizophrenic pitcher, the impulsive hitter, among others. Players like these can be found on just about every major-league team, just about every season.

So this book is about the constants of the game. But it is also very much about change. Baseball has changed enormously since I got into it forty years ago. This book describes some of the most notable developments: the growing importance of video, the decline of base stealing, the sharp drop in complete games, the sharp rise in home runs, and so on. The biggest transformation of all has taken place above players' necks.

In the past, the game was simpler. I am not saying it was easier to be a successful major leaguer, just that there were fewer distractions then. A player's survival was tied primarily to playing as good and as hard as he could. He had to focus on mastering the game's fundamentals, because next year's earnings depended on this year's productivity, and there were several replacements waiting in the minor-league talent pool if you failed to produce. If your team made it to the World Series, your bonus check would provide much-needed extra income.

Now a World Series bonus is little incentive for most players, who earn seven or eight figures a year. Now the pool of potential replacements waiting in the minors is much smaller. Now players' contracts give them the opportunity to earn significant money and security regardless of injury or productivity. Now a player's agent, family, friends, and union encourage him to concentrate on his individual numbers, regardless of how much those stats might contribute to the team's effort to win games, because his personal stats dictate how big his salary will be. Now the players' relationship with the media is contentious and the influence of the players' union overpowering.

Now managers and coaches must battle against all that in persuading their teams to play hard enough and selflessly enough to win ballgames. In spring training and throughout the regular season, we establish and explain the fundamental skills players must master to play the game right. But we spend much more time motivating guys to max out their concentration and effort in practice and competition, convincing them to make winning their first priority. So, in that sense, motivation has become more fundamental than the fundamentals. Even the most selfish player can be inspired to put his team first once he realizes he can gain personally from the club's success. If a club becomes a serious contender, every player earns extra credit that can be cashed in at contract time, because the team's impressive performance makes his own performance look more impressive.

Every successful team has fortune on its side. In each organization where I've managed, good fortune has been a constant teammate. I know of no other manager for whom so many pieces have fallen into place as they have for me. Any manager or coach will tell you that the most essential ingredient of success is quality players, and I've had more than my share of them on the Chicago White Sox, Oakland A's, and St. Louis Cardinals.

I've also been fortunate to work for three franchises whose every level has shown the will and the skill to win. In an era when players' attitudes and relationships to their clubs are so fragile, these three teams have had an edge because their players have sensed this coordinated commitment to win throughout the organization. The standards set by Bill Veeck, Jerry Reinsdorf, and the White Sox ownership; Walter Haas and his family with the A's; and Bill DeWitt and the Cardinals ownership were as high as they get. The front offices of Roland Hemond with the White Sox; Sandy Alderson with the A's; Walt Jocketty with the Cardinals; as well as the coaches, trainers, and everyone associated with those three teams—did their utmost to realize those high standards.

My greatest fortune has been the support of my wife, Elaine, and our daughters, Bianca and Devon. Baseball is very hard on families: No other sport requires so much time on the road. Even when your team's playing at home, you spend roughly twelve hours a day, six days a week at the stadium, so your wife unfairly bears the demands and responsibilities of raising your family. Elaine has borne those burdens better than any man could ask for—with strength, with independence—and to a great degree, I owe the resilience of my family and my success as a manager to her.

PROLOGUE

● ● ● TONY LA RUSSA definitely saw things that kept him up at night: changeups without change, sinkers lacking sink, curves refusing curve. Not to mention the time that Fassero, after being told to throw some garbage nowhere near the plate—bowl it, roll it, slice it, dice it, bounce it if he had to—had thrown it so up and so over that Garciaparra couldn't help but lace it past second to tie the game in extra innings. For four months now, that vision had haunted La Russa, not what Fassero had done but what La Russa *hadn't* done: hadn't adequately prepared Fassero for the moment, leaving Fassero exposed.

The explanation for his sleeplessness was simple, maybe. When anybody does the same thing for as long as he had, going on a quarter century, he was bound to see things he couldn't set aside no matter how hard he tried to rationalize. Another explanation was his own personality: intense, smoldering, a glowing object of glower. He barely smiled even when something wonderful happened, as if he were willing himself not to. Some thought he worked too hard, grinded away at it when he would have been better off forgetting it, took the bad things into the night when he should have slept. Even he knew he had gone too far, had made personal compromises he knew were wrong, but it wasn't simply an occupation to him or even a preoccupation.

It was something he loved. And like other managers who have

spent most of their lives around the game, he had an obsessive mind for it: no at-bat unsung, no pitch ever forgotten, no possibility of simply turning it all off at night. He retained more anecdotes —more memories of balls and strikes and beanballs and stolen signs and games won that should have been lost and games lost that should have been won—than any of the half-pound encyclopedias that came out like clockwork. His meticulous personality accounted only partly for his late-night visions. Maybe the very oddity of his chosen profession was also to blame. Maybe it was the fact that he couldn't simply call an employee in when he had performed badly, couldn't simply talk to him privately. With thousands of people watching, he instead had to walk out and fetch the poor soul as if he were a suicide-in-waiting, then take his weapon away from him because clearly he could no longer be trusted with it, might somehow do further harm than he already had. Or maybe it was all those hand gestures he performed six days a week and sometimes seven: the pantomime of wipes and swipes and scratches.

As much as his job tormented him, he knew that managing a baseball team was a wonderful way to spend a life. It could be thrilling when it went right: when you did something that pushed in a run here and there, when you set up a defense and the ball, often so recalcitrant, obediently played right into the hands of that defense. There was exceptional excitement in the fact that for all the preparation you did, and Tony La Russa was always preparing, the game could never be scripted. As much as he knew—and he had spent his life trying to know—things he never could have imagined still routinely happened, an odd fantastic play that even if it went against you still made you secretly smile in wonder. When the game did work right, hummed along with that perfect hum that every fan recognizes, La Russa would think, simply: "Beautiful. Just beautiful baseball."

If the amount of time he had been at it—the very attitude he had about it—made him something of a throwback, it shouldn't imply that he was simply some tired relic waiting for his retirement papers. No one currently managing had won as many games; he was eighth on the all-time list going into this 2003 season and likely to be as high as third by the time he was finished. No one in the modern history of the game had managed for twenty-four *consecutive* years—starting in 1979 with the White Sox, then with the Athletics, and now with the Cardinals for nearly a decade—an amazing feat of security in a job that had no security. No one else had won the Manager of the Year Award *five* times, across four decades, in both leagues, with each of the three teams he had managed: the White Sox in 1983 when he was still in his Wonder Boy thirties, twice with the Oakland A's in 1988 and 1992 in his forties, and then with the Cardinals in 1996 and 2002.

Along the way, in a game generally terrified of innovation, La Russa, now fifty-eight, had come up with innovations. He had refined the concept of the closer into a one-inning pitcher with the exclusive territory of the ninth. He had made a science of situational matchups between hitter and pitcher in the late innings. (Once he used five pitchers in the space of eight pitches.) And, as if to prove that an obsessive mind was hardly perfect, he had even challenged the hallowed concept of the starting rotation. Briefly, instead of having a single starting pitcher for each game, he went with a starting *grouping* of pitchers in which each one was not allowed to pitch longer than three innings. It was in keeping with his reputation for continual tinkering—too much tinkering in the eyes of some—and it was quietly shelved after a handful of games.

After twenty-four years of managing, it was difficult to imagine that he had ever done anything else. He seemed like someone who had bypassed infancy and childhood and adolescence to appear one day in his chosen profession: He seemed that intimate with it. But he still sensed the intrinsic bizarreness of what he did—the idea of spending his life in what looked like a seedy basement nightclub with a long bench instead of chairs and paper cups instead of shot glasses, a club whose denizens had temperaments as stable as a Silicon Valley IPO. Day in and day out, he had to tell them what to do, even though they made millions more than he did and weren't above back-stabbing betrayal and knew that ultimately, he was a lot more expendable than they were. Even so, he controlled their work schedules, kept them in a game or took them out, got them up or sat them down. As a result, he often humiliated them simply by doing his job. They vented their anger through pouty eyes refusing to look at him from the length of that stark bench. They had pride, enormous pride, at least the ones worth worrying about did. They played with a magic to them that he had never had when he'd played, which made the idea of his telling them what to do—deciding the daily flow of their lives—even more dicey.

He made the decisions he made because of a belief that the whole was always more important than the parts. He likened the team to twenty-five puzzle pieces in which everyone threw his piece in. He kept telling them that, and they nodded when he did, having learned early in their entitled lives that the best way to avoid a lecture was to nod. He told them he loved them, cared about them, needed them. And then he did what he had to do: pinch-hit for them, remove them from that rise of dirt, swap them out for someone with a more reliable glove. And then the next day, he had to tell them all over again how much he loved and needed them.

So it was odd, very odd, perhaps the oddest job in America. As odd as an editor editing his upcoming crop of books on a Central Park bench with all his authors gathered around him fuming over every red line and crossout. As odd as a CEO closing a plant by telling each employee that he had found some workers in India who do it smarter and better and cheaper: In other words, you're all being permanently pinch-hit for, but *don't get me wrong, I still think you're all great!*

Day in and day out, he persevered in the face of the fact that when you're a manager, you never have a 100 percent happy day. There was always something taking away from it, inevitably a burnt ego, somebody who felt scorned or didn't get the start he deserved or the at-bat. He still did the things he had to do, and even when he did them right—knew he had done them right—they still went to hell because the game was eternally mischievous, or "cruel," as he liked to put it, simply cruel. Whether Matt Morris would be able to land on his injured ankle when he pitched: That kept him up at night. The seeming indifference of J.D. Drew, his talent only add-ing to his indifference: That kept him up at night. Kerry Robinson's refusal to follow instructions or stick to fundamentals: That kept him up at night. Trying to figure out what to say to Woody Williams after a particularly heartbreaking loss when he had pitched his brains out: That not only kept La Russa up at night but also had him walking the empty streets of Chicago at 2 A.M. in search of the right words.

Sometimes, he stayed awake to work things out: find an answer in the seeming absence of any, pick a situation apart and put it back together and pick it apart and put it back together again. Beneath his taciturn exterior was an optimist, someone convinced that if you thought about something hard enough, grinded through it enough, examined every possible alternative enough, it could be fixed. That is what happened with the elbow.

The elbow was all he saw at night for a while: not simply anybody's elbow but the elbow of the great Pujols, the best hitter in baseball, even if the only people who knew it for sure at the beginning of 2003 lived in St. Louis. In his first two seasons in the majors, Albert Pujols had hit over .300, driven in more than a hundred runs, and hit more than thirty home runs. And although it was early in 2003, only his third season, he was hitting the ball even better than he had the first two: on his way, if he kept it up, to hitting more than thirty home runs once again and driving in more than a hundred runs once again and *leading* the league in average. It was wonderful for Pujols, obviously, another rapid step up the ladder to pre-emi-nence. But it was also wonderful for the Cardinals: more than won-derful, as their pitching was already in the toilet, with both the starters and the relievers combining to run up the highest ERA in the league. The team couldn't succeed without Pujols's hitting.

And then he injured his elbow on a throw from his position in left field and wouldn't be able to throw with any force for three weeks. In the American League, this wouldn't have been a terrible problem. He couldn't field, maybe, but he still could have his regu-lar place in the batting order; he'd simply be the designated hitter.

But in the National League, in which the dimensions of managing afford far less latitude than in its junior counterpart and therefore far more complication, it meant that Pujols could only pinch-hit until his elbow healed.

This could not have happened at a worse moment. The Cardinals had lost two out of three to Arizona in St. Louis, and Arizona was a down club, hitting poorly, waiting to be plucked. Now the Cardinals were going off on a brutal six-game swing to Atlanta and Florida. Yes, it was only April. But La Russa had learned long ago that April is a great time to push, when most other teams are simply trying to settle in, still trying to figure out whether the puzzle pieces actually amount to anything beyond pieces. He had learned that from Sparky Anderson, and the best proof of that had been the Tigers in 1984 under Anderson's skipperdom, when they had started the season 35–5 on their way to winning a World Series.

So much for this year's April push. But La Russa was worried by the road trip in particular because his team rarely played well in Atlanta. Part of it was psychological, maybe: his nemesis Bobby Cox simply a craggy, crafty old fox who regularly beat him. Part of it was also style: The Braves worked the outside of the plate better than any other team in baseball—made a meal out of it as a matter of policy and instructed pitchers who came over, such as Russ Ortiz from San Francisco, to hit that outside corner for a first-pitch strike, the most important pitch in any at-bat—and then get nasty the rest of the at-bat with a mixture on and off the edges of the plate. He was also worried about the Marlins. He knew that they were stoked with pitching, because he had seen them probably half a dozen times in spring training. The Cardinals would be facing their three right-handed stallions still in the brim of their twenties.

The Cards lost the first game in Atlanta. Then they lost the second when Jeff Fassero, on in relief, just lollipopped one up there, put it right on the plate when the one thing, once again, he should have done was put it off the plate. He made the kind of mistake you maybe expected from a rookie but not from a twelve-year veteran, as if he were *bored* by relieving. And it was unfair to simply single out Fassero, as all the relievers had been ineffective, making fatal mistakes.

After the game, as the team bus made its way to the hotel, La Russa suddenly told the driver to stop. To the players, the game was just another game, a tiny forgotten sliver in the longest season in professional sports. They were in the back of the bus, talking, chirping, making plans for what to do with the night ahead. But La Russa was miserable; losing made him miserable, and being in the suffocating bus made him more miserable. So he got off and walked over to Morton's Steak House just off of Peach Street in downtown Atlanta. It was an odd choice for a strict vegetarian who refuses to eat anything that, as he puts it, once had a face on it. But Morton's was warm and clubby, and given that La Russa lived in a hotel not only when the team played away but also when it played at home, the restaurant was probably as close as he got to the feel of an intimate dining room during the season.

He requested a table for one; after a loss, he liked eating alone. There was no worse social interaction in the complicated history of social interaction than trying to make conversation with Tony La Russa after a defeat, idle chitchat bouncing off a face that with each innocuous and annoying word spoken, looked more and more like a glacier with a migraine. And he wasn't entirely alone, anyway. He at least had his book with him because he always brought a book, potboiler plot, with him when he ate by himself: in this case, James Paterson's *The Jester*, an appropriate title, given what had happened in the ninth to give the Braves the 4–2 win.

He tried to concentrate on *The Jester* as he ate. He flipped through the pages as he simultaneously poked around his salad and his baked potato, but it was of no use. He had worked his way through the tattered bullpen because he had had no choice but to work his way through the tattered bullpen. But as soon as that disturbing vision left, another took its place. Now he fixated on tomorrow's lineup with the lefty Mike Hampton going for Atlanta. When he thought about the lineup, there loomed the elbow of the great Pujols.

Almost as soon as La Russa started managing in the major

leagues in 1979, he discovered that most hitters, like mules in their ruts, hate to be meddled with. They hate trying a new stance or a new swing, even if it may lead to improvement, believing that they must be doing something right to have gotten to where they have gotten. As a result, when someone starts telling them to do this and do that—someone who may have had trouble hitting .200 in the major leagues—they tend not to have a particularly open mind. They operate on the superstition that if they do anything differently—*anything,* from stepping on a chalk line as they approach the batter's box to the mechanics of the swing itself—the delicate assembly line they have concocted will collapse. It's a mindset opposed to that of pitchers, La Russa has also found over the years. Pitchers will experiment with a new pitch daily—throw with their toes, spray it out their butt, flick it off their tongue—if they think it might gain them something.

Because most hitters don't like any change in their routine, lineups are, from a manager's perspective, as much rooted in Freudian analysis as they are in the traditional elements of wanting someone who makes good contact to hit lead-off and putting your power hitters in the middle, and so on and so forth. A manager has to take into account every hitter's whim, superstition, ego, and reality, difficult enough on a good night but on this particular night in the dark wood Jacuzzi of Morton's, further hampered by the glaring absence of Pujols.

Pujols normally batted third, so that was an immediate hole needing to be filled. But it wasn't that simple: Filling Pujols's slot meant changing other hitters' routines, a situation La Russa describes as the "consequences of consequences." Scott Rolen moved to the third spot from his customary fifth position. But Rolen *liked* hitting fifth. He had been flourishing there, so sweetly sandwiched between Jim Edmonds and Tino Martinez. Fifth is where he wanted to be. Fifth is where he should be. La Russa had already moved him to third in the middle of the Arizona series, and his bat had gone silent. So then he had moved Rolen *back* to fifth and put Edgar Renteria in the third spot. But that led only to another consequence of consequence; deep down, Renteria *liked* hitting seventh because he drove in a bunch of runs in that slot.

The lineup was in tatters without the great Pujols: the karmic gestalt of it completely disrupted, a Freudian analysis cut abruptly short, feng shui in crisis. But life is unfair, and La Russa had no choice but to remove an index card from his breast pocket and scratch out a lineup for tomorrow's game. He knew he would give the first baseman Martinez a rest, as it was a day game, and Martinez was an eleven-year veteran who could use the time off after playing the night before. It gave him another hole to fill, and he picked Eddie Perez off the bench to play first. It wasn't a bad choice at all, as Perez, a free swinger, had some pop in the bat.

Then he started thinking about Perez a little bit: The best way to use Perez—to get the most out of him—was to be judicious. He *could* take it deep, which is why he was such a nice player to use off the bench in the late innings and even to start in small doses. But if, in the baseball vernacular, he got too "exposed"—if he was playing so much that pitchers started routinely exploiting the holes in his swing—his effectiveness could be curtailed. So he had to be careful with how much he used Perez.

On the bottom of the little index card he was using to scrawl out his lineup was Pujols's name, alongside the other bench players who might be called on to pinch-hit. With the injured elbow, that's all that Pujols was now: a bench player, a *possible* pinch hitter good for one at-bat. The more he stared at Pujols's name, the more it looked like a waste there at the bottom of the card, on the bench. And then he started thinking about first base, and it hit him: *What about putting Pujols at first base?*

When La Russa had been a player in the 1960s and 1970s, virtually all his career was spent in the minors. He had learned a lot there, perhaps most of all that it was called the minors for a reason. He knew early on, particularly after he hurt his shoulder, that he was never going to have much of a big-league career. He continued to plug away, trying to compensate for lack of talent with drive and hustle, although he knew that these fine and admirable qualities were a poor substitute for it. He also studied: sat on that bench in the dugout, watching managers make moves, wondering why they had made them, and asking afterward why they had made them and refusing to go away until they had given a sufficiently exhaustive answer. He learned from one of his managers, Loren Babe, that in some situations, you have no choice but to sacrifice defense *altogether* to get the offense you need. Babe gave a player in this category—offensive asset, defensive drawback—three at-bats, getting him out of there by the sixth so as not to risk some defensive late-in-game lapse that could not be overcome. That's what led La Russa to the unlikely notion of Pujols at first base.

But Pujols wasn't simply a defensive liability. Because of his elbow, he *couldn't throw* anything beyond a soft toss. It made the idea of playing him at first seem, like many ideas, nice and intriguing and totally impractical, fractured La Russa logic. But he continued to chew on it. He refused to let go of it, convinced that something was still there, something that could still work. What if La Russa played Pujols at first and ordered him *not to throw,* no matter how great the temptation?

He walked from Morton's to the Ritz-Carlton Hotel with a new spring in his step. He got into bed, lay on a skyscraper of pillows, and, naturally, stayed awake. But instead of seeing lollipops over the plate, he now saw an elbow with angel's wings. After he woke up the next morning, he continued to think about it. He thought about it some more on the way from the hotel to the visitor's clubhouse at Turner Field, and when he got to the clubhouse, he found Barry Weinberg, the trainer, to tell him of his scheme.

Weinberg dutifully processed La Russa's scenario and offered a clear and specific reaction—*You can't do it!*—for the obvious reason that if Pujols in the heat of the moment did make a real throw, it could be a career-threatening injury. La Russa listened to Weinberg's reaction. He always listened to Weinberg's reaction because they had been together for nearly twenty years. He was quite fond of Weinberg and sometimes had dinner with him after the team won. He clearly respected Weinberg. And then he called Pujols into the little office.

Pujols was circumspect when he came in, a body language of politeness at odds not only with his 6'4", 225-pound frame but also with the superstar status that with each day was only further entombing him. He was already a great player—maybe the greatest young player the game had seen since Joe DiMaggio and Ted Williams—but he didn't express it with an equal measure of physical arrogance. When La Russa spoke to him about something, he listened because that's what a player was supposed to do.

La Russa started the conversation by asking Pujols who was the best major-league manager he had ever played for. Pujols dutifully answered, "Tony," which was true as well as tactful, as La Russa was the *only* major-league manager Pujols had ever played for.

"We get along good, don't we?" asked La Russa.

"Yes," replied Pujols.

"Well, you know what, you can get me fired by throwing the ball. If you throw the ball, I'll quit."

Pujols nodded that he understood.

"All we have to do is have you lay out for three weeks and you come out 100 percent. So you have to trust me on this strategy, because it gives us a better chance to win."

So Pujols started at first. And it took all of one inning, actually less than that, for the danger of La Russa's scheme to become apparent. In the bottom of the first, Rafael Furcal got on for Atlanta. It brought up Marcus Giles, who tried to sacrifice Furcal to second with a bunt *toward Pujols*. Furcal made it to second, and he could have easily made it to third had he known that Pujols was under orders not to throw the ball. There were no more major episodes at first base after that, but the Cardinals ended up losing to the Braves 4–3 anyway, when the bullpen imploded again and gave up two runs in the bottom of the ninth.

The team dragged into the Westin Diplomat in Miami at about 3 A.M. after the American Airlines charter flight from Atlanta. The players, exhausted, went to bed. But La Russa couldn't sleep. With the three-game sweep by the Braves, the road trip from hell was half done, and the devil seemed in no mood to relent, not with A.J. Burnett and Josh Beckett and Brad Penny pitching for the Marlins: guys who effortlessly threw 94 mph and 95 mph. In his sleeplessness, he began to further examine the Pujols experiment.

Florida was a different team from Atlanta. The Marlins led the league in stolen bases, with Juan Pierre and Luis Castillo, guys who drove you nuts on the basepaths. And with the word trickling out that Pujols couldn't throw—as a baseball dugout was a greater cauldron of gossip than a Flatbush nail salon—La Russa knew there were even more liabilities. A pitcher, for example, couldn't even make a pick-off move to first, because a runner, aware that Pujols couldn't throw properly, would simply take off to second as if it were a free base. So starting Pujols at first was out, particularly as Martinez was coming back into the lineup anyway to face the Marlin trio of right-handers. But then La Russa considered the out-field dimensions in Florida. Left field there was relatively small, with most of the room in center and right. He conjured and pondered—a little bit of this, a little bit of that—until he had another potion.

The next morning, he couldn't wait to try out his newest remedy on somebody. As was his pregame habit, he picked up pitching coach Dave Duncan, bullpen coach Marty Mason, and third-base coach Jose Oquendo in the hotel lobby and they all rode together to the stadium. By now, La Russa was bursting with excitement; on the way there, he told them about his plan to play Pujols in left field and set out the rules he'd devised to make it work:

1. If there's a base hit to left field, Renteria runs out from the shortstop position so Pujols can simply flip the ball to him, which presumably will prevent a runner from trying to stretch a single into a double with the ball in Renteria's glove.
2. If the ball is hit to left center, Pujols fields it and flips it to center fielder Edmonds, who, as Pujols's surrogate, makes the throw back in to prevent an extra base.
3. If a runner on first tries to tag up and go to second on a fly ball to left, Pujols lets him tag up.

Duncan and Oquendo and Mason were receptive. But once in the clubhouse, La Russa had to run the idea past Weinberg because everything involving the players' health had to be run past the trainer. Weinberg's usual answer, based on caution intrinsic to his line of work, was *no,* so La Russa wasn't surprised when Weinberg said that it was an even worse idea than the first-base experiment.

"Tony, he's gonna get hurt. He can't throw."

"I know he can't throw."

La Russa then called the general manager, Walt Jocketty. As it turned out, Jocketty was already aware of his plan. Weinberg, wanting to stop the madness before it became reality, had called him first. But Jocketty became supportive after La Russa convinced him that Pujols, with his intellect for the game, would not give in to any dangerous impulses. It couldn't be said of all players. Maybe it couldn't even be said about most players. But it could be said about Pujols, for whom a nod was more than simply defense against a further lecture.

La Russa knew that it was a risky tactic. He knew that there might be terrible repercussions if it went south, for Pujols and for him. He could be fired if it didn't work: probably *should* be fired because he had jeopardized the exceptional future of an exceptional player. But he also knew that he needed Pujols in the lineup. So he wrote him into left field.

Pujols came up in the top of the first against Burnett. He was hitting third, Rolen fifth, and Renteria seventh. The correct feng shui of the lineup had been restored. Things felt good again. The order of things had been restored. There was a man on first and one out when Pujols settled in at the plate.

He homered on the first pitch. From the corner of his most peculiar office, La Russa whispered the only thing he could possibly whisper: *"Son of a bitch."* Because sometimes it really did work: as it did then, as it must now in the high heat of August—heat born for baseball—with the Cubs coming to town the way every team comes to town this season and all seasons. A three-game series.

cessant seagull screech of the vendors, the out-of-town scoreboard with its inning-by-inning warnings—will have no meaning to him. He won't even be aware of them, as if the game exists for him in a pure extract of silence. He isn't quite in that place yet, and from his office, he occasionally does acknowledge a world outside his own. He scowls when somebody turns up the music in the locker room and a blast of "P.I.M.P." by 50 Cent rages into his office without even as much as a courtesy knock, the decibels so high it would blow the door down anyway. He occasionally peeks at the two television sets that hang at opposite corners from the ceiling of his office: one TV running the satellite feed of Cincinnati playing at Pittsburgh and the other showing an old John Wayne movie, *The Fighting Kentuckians*. "Now that's my kind of movie," he says, but he draws no comfort when Wayne starts to sing. "John Wayne singing. That's nice," he says with misery, momentarily lifting his head from the sheaf of the latest statistics on his upcoming opponent. Then he turns back to the columnar murk of the stats in his ceaseless search for slivery edges, possible aberrations that may be of use during the game.

The stapled packet contains the usual baseball breakdown: at-bats and hits and extra-base hits and walks and strikeouts and average for hitters, wins and losses, and innings pitched and runs allowed and hits allowed and home runs allowed by pitchers. La Russa pays special attention to the individual matchups, an essential ingredient of his approach to managing. These sheets detail how each of his hitters has done against Cubs pitchers and how his pitchers have done against Cubs hitters, as well as the flip side: the individual performances of Cubs hitters against Cardinals pitchers and Cubs pitchers against Cardinals hitters.

The term *bench player* doesn't really apply to the Cardinals, because La Russa so frequently plugs utility players into the lineup based on little opportunities he unearths by sifting through the results of their previous experience with players on the opposing team. These individual matchups are so integral to his strategy that he copies them onto 5-by-7-inch preprinted cards that managers normally use to make out the game's lineup. With ritualistic preci-

GAME
ONE

FEAR FACTOR

I

● ● ● WITH THE SERIES against the Cubs set to beg
in a matter of hours, Tony La Russa is doing what he has d
he first became a major-league manager at the uncerta
thirty-four. He is managing out of fear, preparing as if he
managed before, striving to prove to the world that he
the combination of skills essential to the trade: part tact
psychologist, and part riverboat gambler.

What few words he utters from his office in the bowel
Stadium are less words than they are contorted mumbles
the surface of the floor, you need a fishing net to scoop th
is dressed in Cardinals-red undergarments, and, because
is off to the side of the main locker area, he is oblivious t
ers who trickle in one at a time to eventually get dressed
easygoing and relaxed, all about the sublimation of pr
pretty much a given in baseball—unlike other sports
more hyped you get, the worse off you will be. But La
about pressure.

Tension emanates from his face like a lighthouse be
fog, visible from miles away. He is already moving into
concentration: the tunnel, as he calls it. By game time, h
deep in the tunnel, so riveted on the vagaries of the field
him, that the rest of the spectacle—the swells of the cr

GAME
ONE

....

1

FEAR FACTOR

I

● ● ● WITH THE SERIES against the Cubs set to begin tonight in a matter of hours, Tony La Russa is doing what he has done since he first became a major-league manager at the uncertain age of thirty-four. He is managing out of fear, preparing as if he has never managed before, striving to prove to the world that he possesses the combination of skills essential to the trade: part tactician, part psychologist, and part riverboat gambler.

What few words he utters from his office in the bowels of Busch Stadium are less words than they are contorted mumbles so low off the surface of the floor, you need a fishing net to scoop them up. He is dressed in Cardinals-red undergarments, and, because his office is off to the side of the main locker area, he is oblivious to the players who trickle in one at a time to eventually get dressed. They are easygoing and relaxed, all about the sublimation of pressure. It's pretty much a given in baseball—unlike other sports—that the more hyped you get, the worse off you will be. But La Russa is all about pressure.

Tension emanates from his face like a lighthouse beacon in the fog, visible from miles away. He is already moving into his zone of concentration: the tunnel, as he calls it. By game time, he will be so deep in the tunnel, so riveted on the vagaries of the field in front of him, that the rest of the spectacle—the swells of the crowd, the in-cessant seagull screech of the vendors, the out-of-town scoreboard with its inning-by-inning warnings—will have no meaning to him. He won't even be aware of them, as if the game exists for him in a pure extract of silence. He isn't quite in that place yet, and from his office, he occasionally does acknowledge a world outside his own. He scowls when somebody turns up the music in the locker room and a blast of "P.I.M.P." by 50 Cent rages into his office without even as much as a courtesy knock, the decibels so high it would blow the door down anyway. He occasionally peeks at the two television sets that hang at opposite corners from the ceiling of his office: one TV running the satellite feed of Cincinnati playing at Pittsburgh and the other showing an old John Wayne movie, *The Fighting Kentuckians*. "Now that's my kind of movie," he says, but he draws no comfort when Wayne starts to sing. "John Wayne singing. That's nice," he says with misery, momentarily lifting his head from the sheaf of the latest statistics on his upcoming opponent. Then he turns back to the columnar murk of the stats in his ceaseless search for slivery edges, possible aberrations that may be of use during the game.

The stapled packet contains the usual baseball breakdown: at-bats and hits and extra-base hits and walks and strikeouts and average for hitters, wins and losses, and innings pitched and runs allowed and hits allowed and home runs allowed by pitchers. La Russa pays special attention to the individual matchups, an essential ingredient of his approach to managing. These sheets detail how each of his hitters has done against Cubs pitchers and how his pitchers have done against Cubs hitters, as well as the flip side: the individual performances of Cubs hitters against Cardinals pitchers and Cubs pitchers against Cardinals hitters.

The term *bench player* doesn't really apply to the Cardinals, because La Russa so frequently plugs utility players into the lineup based on little opportunities he unearths by sifting through the results of their previous experience with players on the opposing team. These individual matchups are so integral to his strategy that he copies them onto 5-by-7-inch preprinted cards that managers normally use to make out the game's lineup. With ritualistic preci-